Published by FOWI
fow-i.com
Focus on What's Important, LLC
Racine, WI 53403
Copyright 2021 by Diane Thompson.

All rights reserved.
No part of this book may be reproduced or used in any manner without written permission of the copyright owner except for the use of quotations in a book review.

Written, illustrated and book layout/design
by Diane Thompson.

The illustrations are from artistically enhanced original photographs taken by Diane Thompson.

focus on what's important

created by Diane
fow-i.com

Notes & Acknowledgments

We dug a pond where there was a large field of weeds. It filled naturally with rain and ground water, then we stocked it with fish. Now, we experience the beauty of nature in all forms ~ peaceful.

Thank you Gregg, for your love, encouragement and support. fow-i.com became a reality ~

Live, Love, Laugh...
and enjoy the blessing of Life ;-)

CAN YOU FIND LITTLE GREEN?

This is "Little Green" ~ He is a Green Heron that hides throughout the book.

Can you find him 8 times?

He hides in the book because that is what he does at the Pond.

Hi- it's me, Gwendolyn!
I had no idea how much there was to see outside of the garden!

The ducks, Gretchen and Gus, love showing me around and my favorite place is

THE POND!

The pond is incredible and there are so many bugs!

The first time I visited the pond – I saw a very long legged bird. Gretchen said, "That's Big Blue! He is a Blue Heron and loves to fish near the side of the pond."   Fish?

One day I spotted these two birds and said – HELLO

They looked up.

What are you doing?

"We are looking for fish."

Gretchen and Gus took a bath almost every day. They got all wet and then... shook it off!

Once dry, they spread oil all over their feathers! This made them water proof!

WOW!

BRRR-RUM
 BRRR-RUM
BRRR-RUM

What is that?

When the turkey vultures stopped to catch some sun, Big Blue flew off to give them space. Gretchen told me they were friendly birds and they helped keep the pond shores clean. I wasn't sure how they cleaned, but it was really nice!

One evening, I heard the strangest sounds –
small chirps, then rasping…
a few thumps, and grinding…
a whistle and some peeps.
I flew around the pond looking for the bird,
when I saw a pair of eyes looking up at me
and heard a loud, DEEP… BRRR - R U M

Gretchen laughed and said,
"That's Jumper!" JUMPER?

"Yes, he is a bull frog.
He gets louder at night!" … Oh

peep peep   chirp chirp

Days turned into weeks and other ducks started visiting the pond.

Gretchen said they like to stop for a break. They eat, rest and then...off they go again- on their journey.

They looked different and some went underwater!

What Journey? I thought...

Now- I heard that noise again. This time it was louder.

WHOO WHOOO WHOO WHOOO

Who's there? ~I asked

More ducks stopped and they went underwater too!

They can swim!

Gretchen said they get their food underwater. They eat small fish, bugs, plants and seeds.

They can see underwater and their beaks are long to grip the fish.

I liked it above water, where it was dry~

But it was fun to watch them disappear in one spot and... pop up somewhere else.

I tried to guess where they'd pop up!

I went back to the garden to find my mom. I told her all the things I learned at the pond. She smiled.

"But, I can't find any more bugs." I continued and...
                    I am HUNGRY.

WHOO WHOOO WHOO WHOOO

"Gwendolyn, I love to hear about your adventures- especially DISCOVERING THE POND! You are so enthusiastic." ENTHUSIASTIC?

"Yes, you have great enthusiasm for learning and life! This will help on the journey." WHAT JOURNEY?

"It's time for you to head south, my sweet girl.
It will be warmer and there will be many bugs for you to eat.

It will be one of your GREATEST adventures!

My Inquisitive, Enthusiastic and full of Gumption Girl –
take another Leap of Faith, Gwendolyn…"

Then, mom flew off.

I sat there and thought about everything. I was a little nervous, but also very excited for this big journey.

All of a sudden – Ruby and her brother whizzed past. She stopped to land next to me.

"Hey Gwendolyn! Want to head south with us? We could fly together for a while." YES! YES!

Then, Indy flew down and landed.

"I'll fly with you guys, too!
Gwendolyn... we are going to the same place!"

My tummy did flips with excitement...
ENTHUSIASM!

Where are we going?

to be continued...

Did you find Little Green?
(Here are some clues)

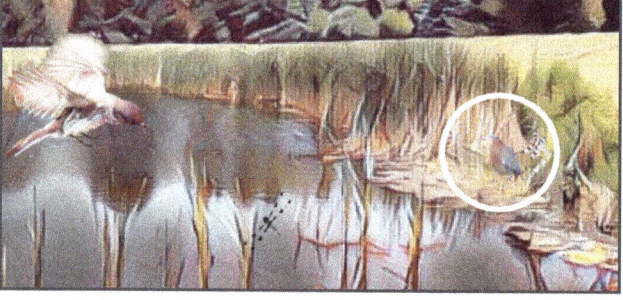

SOME OF THE BIRDS

Bufflehead — Female, Male

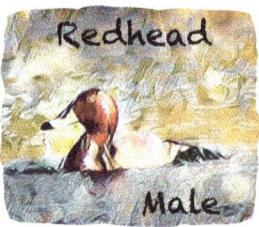

Redhead — Male

Red-breasted Mergansers — Male, Female

Blue-winged Teal — Female, Male

Wood Duck — Female, Male

Common Merganser — Male

Belted Kingfisher — Female, Male

Other books by DEE DEE
INQUISITIVE GWENDOLYN
GWENDOLYN's LEAP OF FAITH
GWENDOLYN finds GUMPTION

Bodacious Bode - The Siberian Husky Pup

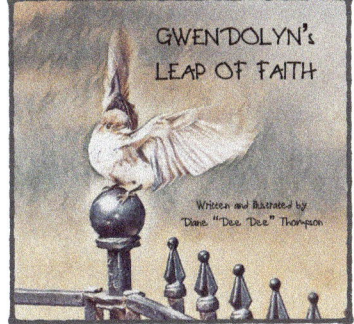

About the Author:

I live in Somers, WI with my husband and dogs, Bode, Jasper & newest member, Jones! My hobby has been photography since I was very young, thus
"Focus" on What's Important. Hope you enjoyed Bode's First three Stories!

For more info, please check out my website.
DEE ♥ DEE

Feel free to connect with me
focus.on.whats.important.77@gmail.com
fow-i.com

Enjoy Animals!   Live - L♥ve - Laugh -
and spend time with others!

CPSIA information can be obtained
at www.ICGtesting.com
Printed in the USA
LVHW052054090921
697442LV00002B/50